FROM SEA to SHINING SEA

WISCONSIN

BETTINA LING

Consultants

MELISSA N. MATUSEVICH, PH.D.
Curriculum and Instruction Specialist
Blacksburg, Virginia

KIFFLIE H. SCOTT, M.S., MLIS
Assistant Youth/Reference Librarian
Maude Shunk Public Library
Menomonee Falls, Wisconsin

KRISTINE STABO, MLS
Youth Librarian
Maude Shunk Public Library
Menomonee Falls, Wisconsin

CHILDREN'S PRESS®
AN IMPRINT OF SCHOLASTIC INC.

New York • Toronto • London • Auckland • Sydney • Mexico City
New Delhi • Hong Kong • Danbury, Connecticut

Wisconsin is in the north central part of the United States. It is bordered by Michigan, Illinois, Iowa, Minnesota, Lake Superior, and Lake Michigan.

Project Editor: Meredith DeSousa
Art Director: Marie O'Neill
Photo Researcher: Marybeth Kavanagh
Design: Robin West, Ox and Company, Inc.
Page 6 map and recipe art: Susan Hunt Yule
All other maps: XNR Productions, Inc.
Consultants: Sharon Durtka and JoAnn Ninham, Milwaukee Public School, Frederick I. Olson

Library of Congress Cataloging-in-Publication Data

Ling, Bettina.
    Wisconsin / by Bettina Ling.
      p.cm. – (From sea to shining sea)
    Includes bibliographical references and index.
    ISBN-10 0-531-18810-8
    ISBN-13 978-0-531-18810-1
    1. Wisconsin – Juvenile literature. I. Title.
F581.3 .L56 2008
977.5—dc22   2007042010

TABLE of CONTENTS

CHAPTER ONE

INTRODUCING THE BADGER STATE

Wisconsin's many dairy cows help make it one of the top producing states of cream, butter, milk, and cheese.

If you like outdoor activities, then Wisconsin is for you. Wisconsin is filled with wonderful natural resources that make it both a vacation paradise and a major agricultural and industrial state.

The name Wisconsin comes from an Algonquian language group word, *Ouisconsin*, that is believed to mean "grassy place," "gathering of the waters," or "place of the beaver." Although the meaning of its name isn't certain, you can find out a lot about Wisconsin from its nickname—America's Dairyland. Wisconsin claims first place nationwide with 26.4 percent of U.S. cheese production. It leads the states in the production of cheddar, Muenster, and Limburger cheeses, and is in second place with other American cheeses and mozzarella. Wisconsin ranks second (after California) in the number of dairy cows. As of August 2007, it had 1,248,000 dairy cows in 14,059 licensed dairy herds. All those cows help Wisconsin produce a lot of dairy products each year, including cheese for more than 78 million people and a one-year supply of milk for nearly 106 million people!

The cow may be Wisconsin's most important animal, but the official state nickname uses the name of another animal, the badger. Wisconsin is known as "the Badger State." The badger is a small mammal with a gray body and a black-and-white head. It lives in burrows—holes or tunnels in the ground. The nickname doesn't come directly from this animal, but rather from the way the lead miners in Wisconsin lived and worked in the 1800s. As they looked for lead, the miners dug tunnels into hillsides just like badgers dig tunnels into the ground.

What comes to mind when you think of Wisconsin?

* Dairy cows on farms in southern Wisconsin
* Fans cheering for the Green Bay Packers football team
* Snowmobile races in Eagle River
* Whitewater rafting down the Peshtigo River
* Harley-Davidson motorcycles being manufactured
* Factories producing cheese
* Hikers enjoying scenic waterfalls
* People of diverse cultures and backgrounds, including Native Americans, African-Americans, Asians, Hispanics, and European immigrants from Germany, Poland, France, Switzerland, and the British Isles

Wisconsin has a rich history and a diverse cultural heritage. Turn the page to discover the story of Wisconsin.

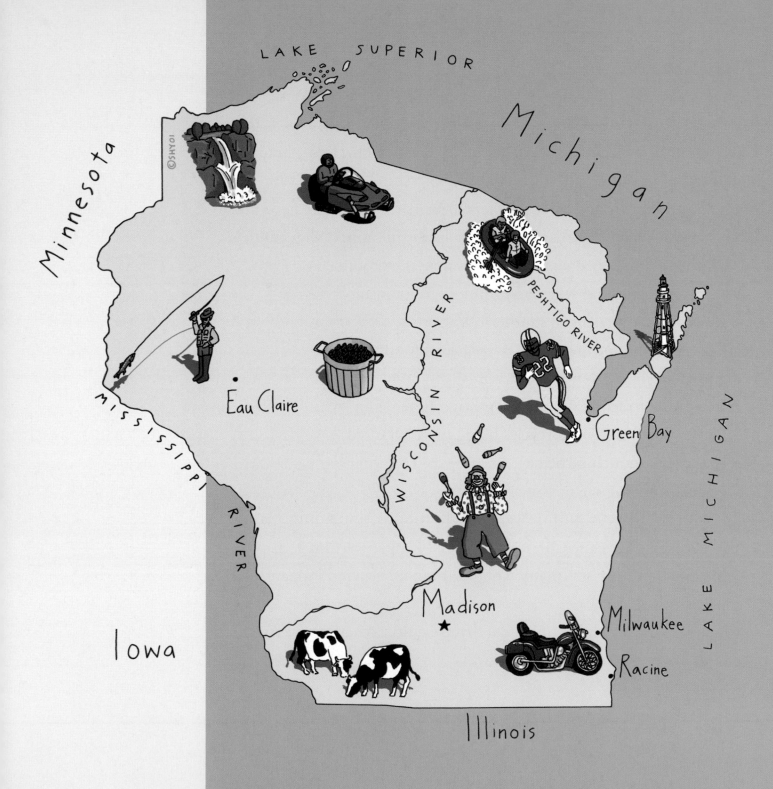

LAKE SUPERIOR

Michigan

Minnesota

©SKY101

MISSISSIPPI RIVER

Eau Claire

WISCONSIN RIVER

PESHTIGO RIVER

Green Bay

LAKE MICHIGAN

Madison
★

Iowa

Milwaukee

Racine

Illinois

CHAPTER TWO

THE LAND OF WISCONSIN

If you look on a map, you'll see that the state of Wisconsin is shaped like a mitten. It is wider at the top, with a long piece of land on the east that sticks out, like the thumb of a mitten, into Lake Michigan. This piece of land is the Door County Peninsula. A peninsula is land that is bounded by water on three sides.

Wisconsin covers 65,498 square miles (169,639 square kilometers). Compared to other states, it ranks twenty-second in size, which makes it a medium-size state. Some of Wisconsin's borders are formed by natural water boundaries. Lake Superior forms some of the northern border, along with the state of Michigan. The Mississippi and St. Croix rivers make up the western border, along with Iowa and Minnesota. Lake Michigan is to the east. The southern border, Illinois, is the only border without water.

Much of Wisconsin's land is perfectly suited for farming.

About one million years ago, the first glaciers—huge sheets of ice and snow—flowed down from the north to cover most of Wisconsin. The movement of the heavy glaciers flattened the hills and filled valleys with rocks and soil. The sliding glacier mass pushed, dragged, and carried rocks and soil along with it, forming hills and big, long ridges of rocks and sand called moraines. In some places, a block of ice was buried under the moraine. It melted slowly and formed a kettle-shaped hole. This process reshaped the surface of the land.

Today, Wisconsin's land is a mix of rolling hills, valleys, ridges, and lakes. There are five geographic regions in Wisconsin: the Lake Superior Lowland, the Northern Highland, the Central Plain, the Eastern Ridges and Lowlands, and the Western Upland (Driftless Area).

The Lake Superior Lowland

The very top of the state is known as the Lake Superior Lowland. This region is hilly with many rivers. It borders the shore of Lake Superior, one of the Great Lakes. Lake Superior is 350 miles (563 km) long and 160 miles (257 km) wide, making it the largest freshwater lake in the world. Lake Superior has surface area of 31,820 sq mi (82,414 sq km), which is almost as big as South Carolina.

The Lake Superior Lowland has very good soil, although not much farming is done there. Even though it lies so far north, the region has a longer growing season than other parts of Wisconsin. Because it borders

(opposite)
One of the best ways to take in the beauty of Lake Superior is to go kayaking. You'll see towering cliffs, sea caves, and rock arches.

the shore of Lake Superior, the Lake Superior Lowland is more protected from the extremes of the cold northern winter.

Off the northern shore are the Apostle Islands. The Apostle Islands National Lakeshore includes twenty-one islands and twelve miles (19 km) of the mainland shoreline. Sandy beaches and sea caves are found on the islands.

Northern Highland

Just south and east of the Lake Superior Lowland is the Northern Highland region. The land in this part of the state contains many lakes, forests, moraines, and rounded hills made of rocks containing iron and copper ore. The soil in this region is very rich. Most of Wisconsin's large forests are in this part of the state.

Some of Wisconsin's most spectacular waterfalls are in this area's two state forests, Chequamegon National Forest and Nicolet National Forest. The Chequamegon National Forest contains the highest point in the state, an area called Timms Hill. It is 1,952 feet (595 meters) high. Both national forests have many hiking and cross-country ski trails.

EXTRA! EXTRA!

Wisconsin has more than 250 cross-country ski trails. One of the state's more challenging trails is Rock Lake Trail, near Cable in the Chequamegon National Forest. It is considered one of the Midwest's most outstanding cross-country ski trails.

Central Plain

Below the Northern Highland lies the Central Plain region. This area is V-shaped and runs from the east border to the west border, dipping down in the central part of the state. It contains several landscapes.

The central and western portions are very flat, while the eastern section has hills and low areas called kettles. Kettles were formed by glaciers. In some places, these kettles contain wetlands or swamps. The soil is sandy, which limits the kinds of plants that grow in this region.

A large gorge called the Wisconsin Dells lies within the Central Plain. A gorge is a deep, narrow passage carved out by glaciers. The Dells is considered one of the most scenic spots in North America, with canyon walls cut in unusual shapes.

The Eastern Ridges and Lowlands

Southeast of the Central Plain lies the Eastern Ridges and Lowlands. The landscape of this region shows the most dramatic effects of the glacier ice. The glacier movement created the land area of Green Bay, as well as the valley of the Rock River and Lake Winnebago. Lake Winnebago is the largest natural lake in the state. It covers 206 square miles (534 sq km).

The northern part of the Kettle Moraine State Forest is in this region. The forest is part of the Kettle Moraine, a long line of beautiful hills with thick forests. It is one of the world's best examples of rock and hill forms created from glacier movement.

This region is one of Wisconsin's best agricultural areas because of its rich soil. Minerals such as iron, copper, and zinc can also be found in the Eastern Ridges and Lowlands area. Most of the larger cities are here, including Milwaukee, the largest city in Wisconsin.

Kettle Moraine State Forest is a popular destination for backpackers.

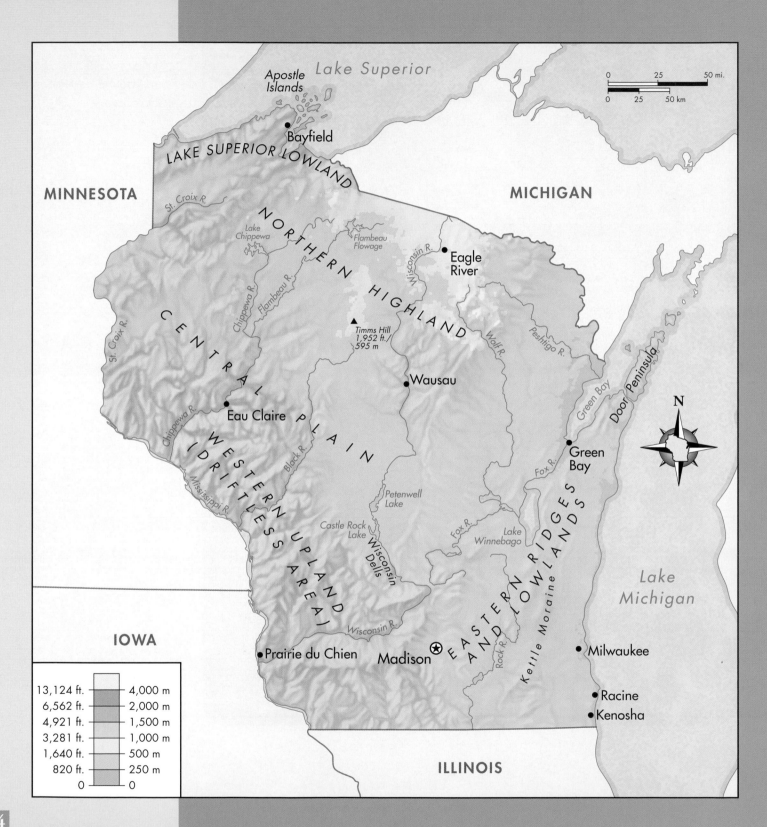

Lake Superior

Apostle
Islands

LAKE SUPERIOR LOWLAND

Bayfield

MINNESOTA

MICHIGAN

St. Croix R.

NORTHERN HIGHLAND

Lake
Chippewa

Flambeau
Flowage

Wisconsin R.

Eagle
River

Chippewa R.

Flambeau R.

CENTRAL

St. Croix R.

Wolf R.

Peshtigo R.

Timms Hill
1,952 ft./
595 m

P L A I N

Wausau

Door Peninsula

Green Bay

N

Chippewa R.

WESTERN

Eau Claire

Black R.

Fox R.

Green
Bay

Mississippi R.

(DRIFTLESS

Petenwell
Lake

Lake
Michigan

UPLAND

Castle Rock
Lake

Fox R.

EASTERN

Lake
Winnebago

RIDGES

Wisconsin
Dells

AREA)

AND

Kettle Moraine

Wisconsin R.

LOWLANDS

IOWA

Prairie du Chien

Madison

Rock R.

Milwaukee

13,124 ft.   4,000 m

6,562 ft.   2,000 m

4,921 ft.   1,500 m

3,281 ft.   1,000 m

1,640 ft.   500 m

820 ft.   250 m

0   0

Racine

Kenosha

ILLINOIS

The Western Upland

In the southwestern part of the state, the Western Upland contains most of what is known as the Driftless Area. It extends up into the Central Plain and the Northern Highland. This region was the only part of the state that was not covered by glaciers, so almost no rock deposits or depressions were left here. The landscape is full of rugged scenery, including cliffs and steep valleys that are not found anywhere else in the state. Rivers cut deep gorges and canyons between the rocks. The Mississippi River forms one of the largest of these gorges.

These sandstone bluffs in Governor Dodge State Park are typical of the rugged scenery in the Driftless Area.

This region has no lakes, but its valleys have rich soil that is good for farming. It also has large deposits of lead and zinc, which were mined by Wisconsin's early settlers.

South of the Wisconsin River are large, hilly areas such as the Military Ridge, the Blue Mounds, and the Baraboo Range. Some of the best views in the state are at the top of these hills.

RIVERS AND LAKES

The many lakes and rivers in Wisconsin provide both water and transportation routes. If you put all the rivers and streams in Wisconsin end to end, they'd stretch nearly 27,000 miles (43,452 km). That's more than enough to circle the whole planet.

The Mississippi River, on the southwest border, is the only river in Wisconsin that commercial ships can travel. Another important river, the Wisconsin, flows southwest for 430 miles (692 km) across the state into the Mississippi. The Wisconsin River flows through the scenic Wisconsin Dells in the middle of the state. The river was an important waterway in pioneer days. Today, there are many dams on the Wisconsin River that use water power to generate energy, or hydroelectricity.

In the western half of the state, the Flambeau, Black, Chippewa, and St. Croix Rivers flow into the Mississippi River. In the north and east, the Menominee, Peshtigo, Wolf, and Fox Rivers flow east into Lake Michigan.

FIND OUT MORE

The waters of Lake Superior and Lake Michigan affect the climate of the land areas around them. As a result, the outer areas of Wisconsin near the lakes are milder in the winter and cooler in the summer than the interior of the state. Why would the lake water affect the temperature of the land around it?

Most of Wisconsin's largest lakes are in the northern and eastern portions of the state. Lake Winnebago is the largest inland lake. It has an area of about 206 square miles (534 sq km). In northeast Wisconsin, the Eagle River Chain of Lakes is the world's largest chain of inland freshwater lakes, with twenty-eight lakes in all. It is one of the biggest fishing areas of Wisconsin. The largest artificial, or manmade, lakes are Petenwell and Castle Rock reservoirs on the Wisconsin River, Lake Chippewa, and the Flambeau Reservoir.

CLIMATE

Wisconsin's climate varies throughout the state. In the north, there are cold winters with mild summers. In the south, there are often hot summers with mild winters.

Throughout Wisconsin, average July temperatures range from more than 72° Fahrenheit (22° Celsius) in the southwest to less than 66°F (19°C) in some northern areas. Daytime temperatures are usually not much higher than 90°F (32°C). January temperatures average below freezing throughout most of the state.

Rainfall is heaviest during the spring and summer. The average annual rainfall ranges from 28 to 32 inches (71 to 81 centimeters). The amount of snowfall varies from about 30 inches (76 cm) in the southern part of the state to well over 100 inches (254 cm) in northern Wisconsin.

CHAPTER THREE

WISCONSIN THROUGH HISTORY

In this area now called Wisconsin, the first peoples constructed wigwams and lived in settlements.

EXTRA! EXTRA!

Before Paleo-Indians, the first living things in Wisconsin were tiny creatures called trilobites. Trilobites were small marine animals that looked like a cross between a bug and a crab. They lived in a huge saltwater sea that covered much of Wisconsin about a half-billion years ago. Today, their fossils can be found throughout most of Wisconsin. They became the official state fossil in 1985.

The first people came to the area that is now Wisconsin more than 12,000 years ago. They were Paleo-Indians who followed large game animals, including mammoths, into the region. Mammoths were huge beasts up to fourteen feet (4 m) high, with trunks and long tusks. They lived on the rich plant life in Wisconsin. Paleo-Indians lived in small groups, moving their settlements from place to place. They followed their food supply, tracking and hunting animals, fishing, and gathering nuts, wild plants, and berries for food.

Around 800 B.C., the descendants of these first humans, called the Woodland people, formed larger groups that lived together in settlements. They created bows and arrows to hunt animals. During this period, a new group of Native Americans, the Hopewell people, came to the Wisconsin region to trade with the people living there. These cultures built earth mounds throughout southern Wisconsin. The late Woodland culture made effigy mounds, which were shaped like animals. Some may have been places of worship, and others may have been places to bury the dead. Only a few of these mounds remain today in Wisconsin.

Close to A.D. 1200, people from other cultures also lived in Wisconsin. The Mississippean and Oneota civilizations lived mainly in southern Wisconsin. The Oneota lived in settlements. Much of what we know about them comes from paintings and carvings that were done on cave walls in the Driftless Area. Some of these pictures can be seen today. They include human and animal figures.

Some early Native American mounds were preserved and can be seen at Aztalan State Park.

Some of the earliest nations in Wisconsin were the Ho-Chunk (Winnebago), Dakota, and Menominee. By the 1600s, new Native American groups moved into Wisconsin, including the Wyandot (Huron), Anishinaabe (Ojibwe), Odawa (Ottawa), Petun, Sauk, Meskwaki (Fox), Kickapoo, Mascouten, Potawatomi, and Illinois.

Native American groups lived in villages and towns of several hundred people. Many of the Native Americans in Wisconsin lived in dome-shaped structures called wigwams. These were made of saplings covered with bark or woven mats. They fished and grew some crops for food, such as corn and beans. Native Americans used wild rice found in river valleys as one of their main foods. In winter, these villages would split up into small hunting parties that hunted buffalo and other animals for meat and clothing.

ARRIVAL OF THE EUROPEANS

In the early 1600s, a French explorer named Jean Nicolet was traveling with other Frenchmen in the western Great Lakes area. They were looking for a faster route across the middle of North America to Asia. In 1634 the Huron took Nicolet to meet the Ho-Chunk at Red Banks near Green Bay, making him one of the first Europeans to set foot in Wisconsin.

Nicolet soon learned that the area was rich in valuable natural resources. One of the most valuable was animal fur. At that time, people in Europe used beaver furs to make coats and hats. When Nicolet returned to Canada, he told people about all the rich natural resources

in Wisconsin. Word spread throughout Europe, and many Europeans came to the Wisconsin area looking for furs.

Europeans enlisted the help of Native Americans in Wisconsin, who were especially skilled at hunting and trapping. The Ojibwe, in particular, were well suited to the fur trade. They followed a pattern from one season to the next, fishing in the summer, harvesting wild rice in the fall, and

This drawing shows Jean Nicolet meeting the Ho-Chunk at Red Banks in Green Bay.

Many fur trappers came to the Wisconsin area, hoping to strike it rich.

hunting, trapping, and fishing in the winter. They transported their homes each time they moved. Native Americans traded with the Europeans for cloth, metal tools, kettles, jewelry, and guns, in exchange for furs, deer meat, corn, and wild rice.

One well known French trader was Nicolas Perrot, who came to Wisconsin in 1667. He established a series of trading posts. The post at Green Bay became a center for the Wisconsin fur trade. In 1689, Perrot claimed the Upper Mississippi Valley, including what is now Wisconsin, for France.

Along with the fur traders, French settlers and missionaries came to Wisconsin. The settlers started farms. The French missionaries were priests who wanted to share their Christian beliefs with the people in this new land.

The valuable fur trade of the region also attracted trappers from England. By the early 1700s, France and England were fighting over control of Wisconsin and other territories in North America. This soon led to the French and Indian War (1754–1763), fought between the French and the British

(English). Some Native Americans fought on the French side because they had established trade relationships with them. Others fought on the English side.

As a result of the war, the French lost their claim to these lands. A treaty, or agreement, was signed in which all French territories east of the Mississippi River, including Wisconsin, were given to Britain. The British and some French continued to use Wisconsin as a center for their fur trade industry for the next twenty years. Green Bay, La Pointe, and Prairie du Chien became important posts for the British fur trade.

During this time the British also controlled colonies, or settlements, in the east along the Atlantic Coast. Although they were far from Wisconsin, the colonies would prove to be important to its development. In 1775,

The French and Indian War was largely about gaining control of the fur trade in the New World.

after many years of living under British rule, some colonists became dissatisfied. They wanted to form their own, independent country. In an effort to gain freedom, they rebelled against Britain and fought a war called the American Revolution (1775–1783).

Colonists, along with their Native American allies, fought against the British soldiers, mostly on the East Coast and in the South. The colonists and their allies won the war and as a result, the colonies became an independent nation. A formal agreement known as the Treaty of Paris gave the United States all of Britain's territory east of the Mississippi River, north to Canada, and south to the border of Spanish Florida. The land that later became known as the state of Wisconsin was now controlled by the United States.

In 1787, the United States government organized a large section of land into what was known as the Northwest Territory, which included Wisconsin. Even though the United States claimed the land, Britain maintained its hold on the fur trade in Wisconsin and refused to leave the area. The British urged Native Americans to attack American settlers who moved to the area in an attempt to drive them away. In 1812 a war broke out again between the United States and Britain. When the war ended, the British finally agreed to stay out of the Northwest Territory, including Wisconsin.

In the 1820s, word spread of a major lead-ore discovery in Wisconsin near New Diggings, Hazel Green, and Shullsburg. At the time, lead was used to make bullets for weapons. This exciting news brought another group of people to Wisconsin—miners. Wisconsin was rich in deposits of lead, zinc, and iron. Diamonds, too, were found at different places in the state. One of the most famous was the Eagle Diamond, discovered in 1876 in Eagle, Wisconsin. It weighed about 16 carats and is one of the largest diamonds uncovered in Wisconsin. Several major lead discoveries were made in southwestern Wisconsin, which helped to make this area one of the most important lead production areas in the country. By 1829, there were about 10,000 miners and many mines in the region.

More miners moved in and disrupted the settlements of Native Americans. As their land gradually disappeared, Native Americans began to fight back to defend their homes and lands. They attacked miners and their families. To protect the settlers, the United States government built Fort Crawford in Prairie du Chien.

In 1825, the United States government called a meeting with representatives from some of the Wisconsin and Illinois Native American nations. Native Americans were forced to sign treaties, or formal agreements, requiring them to sell or trade their land to the government. Many tribes were moved across the Mississippi River to Iowa and other places.

FIND OUT MORE

In the early 1700s, Britain, France, and Spain all claimed parts of North America from Canada through the Great Lakes and down to the Gulf of Mexico. Create a map showing the North American territories of each country at that time.

The Black Hawk War was devastating for the Fox-Sauk.

In 1832, a large group of Fox-Sauk returned to the state of Illinois. What began as a peaceful mission turned into the Black Hawk War. After this war, more treaties were signed and the United States government forced more Native Americans in Wisconsin to move away to other areas. Some groups, through treaties, were able to keep parts of their home territory. Some Ho-Chunk were forced to move and when they returned they had to buy back their land. In central and northern Wisconsin, land was set aside for Indian use. These areas were called reservations.

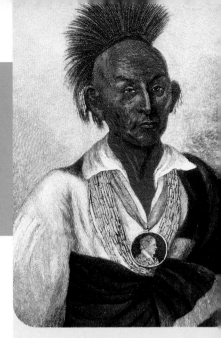

THE TERRITORY OF WISCONSIN

In 1836, the United States Congress made the Wisconsin area a separate region called the Territory of Wisconsin. Colonel Henry Dodge was named governor. He chose the town of Belmont as Wisconsin's first capital. However, the needs of the capital quickly outgrew Belmont, and in 1838 the capital was moved to the larger city of Madison. Madison is still the capital today.

Loggers came to Wisconsin in the 1820s, making logging one of the territory's chief sources of income. Cut timber was used to build houses and buildings, and to make paper products. Sometimes it was loaded onto ships or trains and sent to other cities, such as Chicago. The Menominee, a Native American nation in Wisconsin, also built a successful lumber industry in the northeastern part of the territory.

Settlers from other parts of the United States, as well as from Europe, came to Wisconsin, including people from Germany, Norway, Sweden, and Switzerland. These new settlers were interested in buying land to create cities, or to begin farming. Farmers grew oats and wheat. By the 1840s, wheat had become the principal crop. Many miners turned to farming, as well. By 1845, most southwestern mines were stripped bare of lead. Some miners left for California after gold was discovered there in 1848.

Early settlers, mostly farmers, had a hard life. They made most of the things they needed to live, such as soap, candles, clothing, and shoes.

They grew the food they ate. They had to clear the woods to build small wooden cabins. One German settler described his home in these words, "Our log house at present consists of only one room, which I shall later transform into two. . . . It is one and a half stories high. . . . We get to our bedroom on the second floor with the help of a ladder, having yet had no time to build stairs. . . . "

Everyone in the family worked, including the children. Pioneer life could be very lonely, because the nearest neighbors and towns were miles away. Winters, especially, were long and hard. Snowstorms could leave huge snow piles that stranded a family inside their cabin for weeks.

WHAT'S IN A NAME?

The names of many places in Wisconsin have interesting origins.

Name	Comes from or means
Wisconsin	Algonquian language word meaning "gathering of the waters," "place of the beaver," or "grassy place"
Madison	James Madison, fourth president of the United States
Green Bay	From French words La Baye Verte, or "the green bay"
Platteville	"Platts," bowl-shaped masses of melted lead made by Native Americans
La Crosse	Native American game played with long-handled racquets that look like crosses
Eau Claire	French words meaning "clear water"
Wisconsin Dells	From French word dalles, or slab-like rock; or Anishinaabe word meaning "where the dark, rushing waters meet"

STATEHOOD AND THE CIVIL WAR

By the late 1840s, there were about 300,000 people living in the Territory of Wisconsin, most of whom were farmers. The people wanted their region to become a state. On May 29, 1848, Wisconsin was admitted to the Union as the 30th state. Its first elected governor was Nelson Dewey.

As Wisconsin's population grew, the state built better transportation routes. In 1851, Wisconsin's first railroad, built by the Milwaukee & Mississippi Railroad Company, began when a passenger train took a twenty-mile (32-km) trip from Milwaukee to Waukesha. In 1857 the railroad was completed. It connected Milwaukee in the east to Prairie du Chien in the west.

During the mid-1800s the United States, too, was growing. However, the northern states and southern states were following different paths. In the South, many people used African-Americans as slaves, forcing them to work on large farms called plantations. Slaves were owned by the white people they worked for. They had no freedoms and were frequently harshly punished for disobeying their masters. Most slaves were not allowed to learn how to read and write, nor could they own property. The southern states were known as slave states.

Most northern states were known as free states. It was illegal to own slaves there. In the North, people often worked in factories or mills where they were paid wages for their work. Many people in the North thought that slavery was wrong. Wisconsin was a free state. The African-Americans who lived in Wisconsin were free people.

Many people spoke out against slavery, and some even helped slaves to escape through the Underground Railroad. This was not a train, but a chain of people who helped slaves escape from the South into the free states or Canada. In Wisconsin, a

FIND OUT MORE

People in many states secretly participated in the Underground Railroad. Write a short biography about a famous person or place in any state that was part of the Underground Railroad.

man named Joseph Goodrich owned an inn called Milton House, which was a famous stop on the Underground Railroad.

Many slaves escaped to the North, and southerners became angry. They worked to create a law that made it legal for slave owners to chase and capture their runaway slaves. Once captured, slaves would be forced to return to their harsh lives. This was called the Fugitive Slave Act.

Most Wisconsin citizens did not like the Fugitive Slave Act. This law was tested in the Wisconsin courts with the case of a runaway slave named Joshua Glover, whose owner tried to get him back. The Wisconsin Supreme Court declared the law unconstitutional.

When Abraham Lincoln was elected president in 1860, he wanted to abolish, or put an end to, slavery in the United States. The southern states believed that each state should decide on its own whether to end slavery. In protest of Lincoln's plan, the southern states seceded, or broke away from, the United States. They formed their own nation called the Confederate States of America. The tension between the two sides led to the Civil War (1861–1865).

Wisconsin joined the other northern states in the war, sending almost 96,000 soldiers and other volunteers. Much of the fighting took place in the South. At home, women took over the farm and factory work. Wisconsin women formed the Soldier's Aid Society and supported the soldiers by serving as nurses. They sent soldiers packages filled with cookies, jellies, meats, and letters from home. In 1865, the North won the Civil War.

AFTER THE WAR

The war brought many changes to Wisconsin. While the men were away fighting in the war, women worked. Afterward, more women worked in places outside their homes such as factories, stores, and offices. People began moving into the state to work in the industries that had started during the war. Milwaukee went from a city of 50,000 people to a city of 265,000 people in only a few decades.

Milwaukee became a bustling place by the early 1900s. This illustration shows the Grand Avenue Bridge and Wisconsin Street, now Wisconsin Avenue.

In the years after the war, the first civil rights laws were created in Wisconsin. Although African-Americans were no longer slaves in the South, they were still not seen as equal citizens. Many states discriminated against them and created laws to keep them from having the same rights as white people. Wisconsin passed a civil rights law in 1895 that made it illegal to discriminate against any person.

During this time, one of the deadliest forest fires in the history of the United States occurred in the logging region of Wisconsin. The summer of 1871 had been hot with little rain. On October 8, in the town of Peshtigo, dry plants and grasses ignited into flames from the heat of the sun. High winds fanned the flames, setting ablaze piles of sawdust and cut wood.

Later, a survivor wrote about what he saw: "The air was a blizzard of burning coals igniting all they touched. . . . In less than twenty minutes, all that could be seen for miles were swirling smoke and coils of flame." When it was over, the Great Fire of Peshtigo had destroyed the entire town and taken the lives of more than one thousand people.

During the second half of the 1800s, farming became important in the state. Many farmers converted to dairy farms instead of growing crops. A number of Wisconsin farmers were from European countries such as Switzerland and Norway, where lots of cheese was cheese was made. At first, these farmers began making cheese as a way to preserve excess milk. It wasn't long, however, before cheese was produced and sold on a larger scale. In 1864, the first cheese factory was started at Ladoga by Chester Hazen. Cheese helped make Wisconsin a major dairy state. After an invention called the cream separator came into use, butter was also made in factories.

By the early 1900s, many of Wisconsin's great pine forests had been cut down by the lumber industry. Old forestland became dairy farms. Manufacturing businesses started making heavy machines needed for farming and other industries. Many African-Americans from the South moved to Wisconsin to work in manufacturing plants in cities such as Racine, Beloit, and Milwaukee.

In 1900, Wisconsin's population reached over two million and was incredibly diverse. In the census that year, seven of every ten people in the state reported that either they or their parents were born in a foreign country. For the first time, however, a Wisconsin-born governor, Robert M. La Follette, was elected in 1900.

In 1917, America entered World War I (1914–1918), just a year before it ended. Wisconsin sent soldiers, doctors, and nurses to the war in Europe. Nearly 125,000 Wisconsinites served as soldiers.

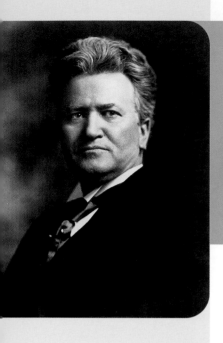

Farms increased food production to feed the troops. Wisconsin factories made machinery and transportation vehicles for the war. Ships and submarines were built in cities near the Great Lakes. Manitowoc and Superior became major shipbuilding cities. When the war ended in 1918, the manufacturing industries that had been started during the war continued on in Wisconsin.

PIONEERS OF SOCIAL CHANGE

During this time, American women wanted an amendment to the constitution that granted them suffrage. Suffrage means the right to vote. Women who fought for this cause called themselves suffragettes. Many leading suffragettes were from Wisconsin, including Carrie Chapman Catt and Mathilde Anneke. In 1920, the Nineteenth Amendment was passed and women were granted voting rights.

In 1929, the United States entered a period that was known as the Great Depression. Many people lost money they had invested in the stock market. Wages were low, but the price of goods was high, so people couldn't afford to buy things they needed. Companies made more products than they could sell. As a result, companies lost money and had to reduce the number of workers. Many businesses closed. This was a very hard time for all the states, including Wisconsin. Millions of people lost their jobs. Wisconsin's farming industry suffered when the price of crops went down. Farmers couldn't earn enough money, and many lost their farms.

In 1930, Philip F. La Follette, son of Robert La Follette, was elected governor. Under his administration, thousands of Wisconsin residents were given jobs on projects such as building roads and creating parks. People began earning money again. In 1932, the Wisconsin legislature passed the nation's first unemployment compensation law. This law gave funds to people when they lost their jobs. It also helped them pay their bills while they looked for work. The law served as a model for other states as well as for the United States government. Wisconsin also pioneered a number of other social reform laws that are used today throughout the country.

FAMOUS FIRSTS

- Margarethe Meyer Schurz opened the country's first kindergarten in Watertown, 1856
- Ed Berner's soda fountain in Two Rivers served the first ice-cream sundae, 1878
- The nation's first automobile race took place in Wisconsin, 1878
- The first performance of the Ringling Brothers Circus took place in Baraboo, 1884
- Carl Eliason invented the snowmobile in Sayner, 1924
- The Green Bay Packers won the first Super Bowl, 1967

The beginning of World War II (1939–1945) helped America recover from the Great Depression. Extra goods, machinery, and food were needed for the war. People found jobs and spent money. In Wisconsin, manufacturing companies and farms started doing well again. Wisconsinites also helped fight the war—300,000 citizens served as soldiers, and 7,980 soldiers died.

After the war, manufacturing became Wisconsin's main economic activity, though agriculture continued to do well for the next twenty years.

In the 1950s and 1960s, there were still many states that discriminated against African-Americans, Native Americans, and Hispanics, and people were angry about this unfair treatment. Civil rights demonstrations took place on several college campuses in Wisconsin. In summer 1967, a riot by angry African-Americans occurred in Milwaukee, and one person was killed.

Many African-Americans and other people worked to get these unfair practices changed. In Milwaukee, African-Americans filed lawsuits to end segregation, the practice of placing black children in separate schools from white

WHO'S WHO IN WISCONSIN?

Carrie Chapman Catt (1859–1947) was a leader in the suffragist movement. After the Nineteenth Amendment was passed, she was one of the founders of the National League of Women Voters and served as its first president. She was born in Ripon.

children. In 1976 a federal court ordered schools to desegregate, forcing them to end the separation.

Wisconsin's economy began to weaken in the 1970s. Many dairy farmers went out of business due to the rising cost of producing milk. Large companies (or "corporate" farms) took over dairy farms, and the family dairy farms of Wisconsin began to disappear. By the 1990s, California had surpassed Wisconsin as leader of the dairy industry.

Native Americans in Wisconsin also continued to fight the state to uphold their treaty rights. The state government had long outlawed spearfishing, a traditional Native American activity. In 1983, a federal court stated that Native Americans had the right to fish. This decision sparked much controversy, because most people saw spearfishing as a threat to Wisconsin's fish resources. Finally, in 1991, the Wisconsin Ojibwe won a legal battle against the state government which upheld their treaty rights to fish, hunt, and gather within the ceded territory.

Although the number of dairy farms in Wisconsin decreased in the 1970s, the remaining farms tended to increase in size.

Many people flock to the casinos, which have generated money for some Native American groups in Wisconsin.

An important economic change occurred for some of the Wisconsin Native American nations when they opened casino gambling businesses in the 1980s and 1990s. Casinos increased the income for some Native American nations, particularly the Potawatomi nation, one of the most economically successful in the state. Often, these casinos are the largest employer in the area, providing jobs for some Native Americans and other people living near the casinos. They also provide money for Native Americans' education, health, and cultural programs. However, many Native Americans still struggle with poverty and unemployment.

The expansion of manufacturing in Wisconsin in the late 20th century was good for the state's economy but sometimes bad for its environment. Manufacturing plants depleted the state's natural resources and created pollutants that threatened tourism and dairy farming. As a result, Wisconsin citizens have worked at creating better laws and programs to protect the environment. The state passed a major recycling law in 1990. Today, Wisconsin continues its efforts to protect the environment with the help of new educational programs.

After more than 150 years as a state, Wisconsin is still a driving force for economic and social change. Wisconsin is a leader in fish and wildlife conservation. The state has also pioneered the replanting of trees on forest land that has been devastated by destructive logging practices. Wisconsin also works at creating change in social services and health care. Changes like these pave the way to a bright future for both Wisconsin and the United States.

WHO'S WHO IN WISCONSIN?

Gaylord Nelson (1916–) was born in Clear Lake. He is a former governor and United States senator from Wisconsin. He sponsored many conservation bills to preserve wilderness areas. He also received the nation's highest civilian award, the Presidential Medal of Freedom, for founding Earth Day. Earth Day calls national attention to the environment, and is celebrated on April 22nd.

CHAPTER FOUR

GOVERNING WISCONSIN

Wisconsin's state capitol is located between Lake Mendota on the west and Lake Monona on the east.

(opposite)
Legislators gather inside the state capitol to hear a speech by the governor.

Wisconsin still uses essentially the same constitution it adopted at the time of statehood in 1848. A constitution is a document that defines how a nation, state, or group is organized. The Wisconsin constitution states the rights of its citizens and also determines the powers of its government. It is one of the oldest state constitutions in the United States. An amendment, or change to the constitution, must be approved by a majority of the people who vote on it. Wisconsin's government is made up of three branches, or parts—legislative, executive, and judicial.

EXECUTIVE BRANCH

The executive branch enforces and carries out the laws of the state. The governor is the head of the executive branch. He or she is elected by the people of Wisconsin. The governor is elected every four years and can run for an unlimited number of terms.

Other members of the executive branch include the secretary of state, the lieutenant governor, the state treasurer, the attorney general, and the superintendent of public instruction. All these elected officials work together with the governor to help run the state.

LEGISLATIVE BRANCH

The job of the legislative branch is to create laws to help the people of Wisconsin. For example, legislators might make laws that protect the environment, help pay for schools, or build roads. They also create the state budget to determine how money will be spent to run all the services of the state.

The Wisconsin legislature is divided into two houses—the assembly and the senate. The assembly has ninety-nine members. Each member is elected by the people of Wisconsin to serve a two-year

term. There are thirty-three senators. Each senator is elected for a four-year term.

JUDICIAL BRANCH

The judicial branch is made up of courts and judges. Their job is to interpret or determine the meaning of laws. The court system decides whether someone has broken the law and also determines the punishment. If two parties disagree over a law, the courts make the final decision.

Municipal courts are city courts. Most minor cases, such as traffic violations, are heard in municipal courts. Municipal judges are elected to four-year terms.

Circuit courts hear more serious cases, such as criminal trials and cases involving children. They are the main trial courts in Wisconsin. If a person is unhappy with the decision that was reached in circuit court, they can take their case to a higher court, the court of appeals. Judges in both circuit courts and the court of appeals are elected for six-year terms.

The highest court in Wisconsin is the state supreme court. The job of the supreme court is to review decisions made in certain cases in the lower courts. The supreme court is also in charge of the entire Wisconsin court system. The supreme court is made up of seven justices who are elected for ten-year terms. The justice with the longest service on the supreme court serves as its chief justice.

WHO'S WHO IN WISCONSIN?

William Rehnquist (1924–2005) was born and raised in Milwaukee. He has served as an associate justice on the United States Supreme Court since 1971. In 1986 he was appointed Chief Justice.

WISCONSIN STATE GOVERNMENT

EXECUTIVE BRANCH

Governor

Lieutenant Governor

Secretary of State

Attorney General

State Treasurer

Superintendent of Public Instruction

LEGISLATIVE BRANCH

Senate

Assembly

JUDICIAL BRANCH

Supreme Court

Courts of Appeal

Circuit Courts

Municipal Courts

WISCONSIN GOVERNORS

Name	Term	Name	Term
Nelson Dewey	1848–1852	Emanuel Philipp	1915–1921
Leonard Farwell	1852–1854	John Blaine	1921–1927
William Barstow	1854–1856	Fred Zimmerman	1927–1929
Arthur MacArthur	1856	Walter Kohler Sr.	1929–1931
Coles Bashford	1856–1858	Philip La Follette	1931–1933
Alexander Randall	1858–1862	Albert Schmedeman	1933–1935
Louis Harvey	1862	Philip La Follette	1935–1939
Edward Salomon	1862–1864	Julius Heil	1939–1943
James Lewis	1864–1866	Walter Goodland	1943–1947
Lucius Fairchild	1866–1872	Oscar Rennebohm	1947–1951
Cadwallader Washburn	1872–1874	Walter Kohler Jr.	1951–1957
William Taylor	1874–1876	Vernon Thompson	1957–1959
Harrison Ludington	1876–1878	Gaylord Nelson	1959–1963
William Smith	1878–1882	John Reynolds	1963–1965
Jeremiah Rusk	1882–1889	Warren Knowles	1965–1971
William Hoard	1889–1891	Patrick Lucey	1971–1977
George Wilbur Peck	1891–1895	Martin Schreiber	1977–1979
William Upham	1895–1897	Lee Dreyfus	1979–1983
Edward Scofield	1897–1901	Anthony Earl	1983–1987
Robert La Follette	1901–1906	Tommy G. Thompson	1987–2001
James Davidson	1906–1911	Scott McCallum	2001–2003
Francis McGovern	1911–1915	Jim Doyle	2003–

TAKE A TOUR OF MADISON, THE STATE CAPITAL

Although Madison is Wisconsin's second-largest city, it has the charm of a small town. More than 200,000 people live in Madison, many in small communities with a particular ethnic heritage. It is one of the nation's most scenic cities, with 200 parks and four lakes, making Madison one of the country's top canoeing towns.

State Street connects the capitol and the University of Wisconsin. It is lined with shops and restaurants.

Madison became the capital of Wisconsin in 1838, and the first capitol building quickly became too small. In 1863 it was replaced by a larger building, which was badly damaged by fire less than fifty years later. The present capitol building was built between 1906 and 1917.

The new capitol building, located in the center of Madison, was modeled after the nation's Capitol in Washington, D.C. On the ceiling of the rotunda, the large round room inside the entrance of the capitol, is a mural showing Wisconsin's natural resources. The capitol dome is made of white Vermont granite and is topped by a bronze statue of a woman that was named for the state's motto, "Forward." Wisconsin's capitol is 286 feet (87m) high. It is taller than any other capitol building except the national Capitol in Washington, D.C.

On Saturday mornings May through October, the farmers' market is the place to be.

For much of the year, the area around the capitol building, called Capitol Square, is turned into a huge open-air market with the arrival of the Dane County Farmers' Market. Every Saturday, local farmers sell everything from lettuce to freshly made summer sausage and cheese.

In other parts of the city you'll find historical buildings that were designed by famous Wisconsin architect Frank Lloyd Wright.

One of Wright's buildings is directly south of the capitol, on the edge of Lake Monona. The Monona Terrace Community and Convention Center holds meetings, banquets, and other events for the local community.

From the capitol, take a walk down State Street. This street is filled with interesting shops, restaurants, museums, and galleries. State Street will lead you to the University of

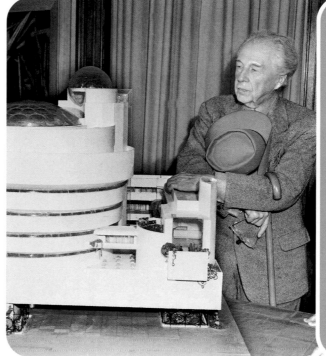

Wisconsin, located on the opposite end of town. You can visit several museums on campus, including the Geology Museum, which has a fascinating collection of rocks and fossils. There are also plenty of places on campus to enjoy outdoor activities, such as walking or bicycling. A greenhouse and gardens are open for tours.

There are lots of other things to see and do around Madison. The Henry Vilas Zoo has all kinds of animals, from giraffes and camels to kangaroos and penguins. The zoo's Discovery Center gives you a chance to see things up close—including the details of a screech owl's skull and the skin of a python! Afterward, stop at the zoo's beach on the shore of Lake Wingra, where you can relax in the sun.

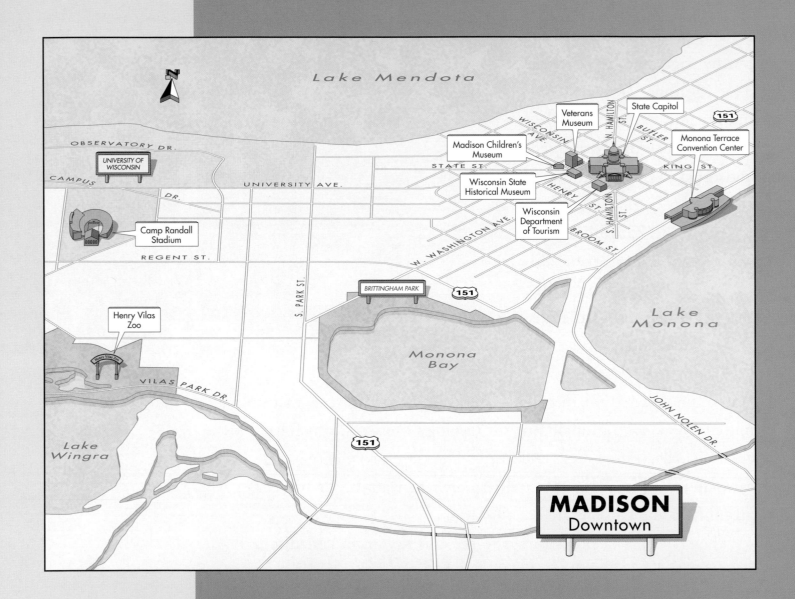

N

Lake Mendota

OBSERVATORY DR.

UNIVERSITY OF WISCONSIN

CAMPUS

DR.

UNIVERSITY AVE.

STATE ST

WISCONSIN AVE

Veterans Museum

Madison Children's Museum

State Capitol

151

Monona Terrace Convention Center

Wisconsin State Historical Museum

N. HAMILTON ST.

BUTLER ST.

KING ST.

HENRY ST.

Wisconsin Department of Tourism

S. HAMILTON ST.

BROOM ST.

Camp Randall Stadium

REGENT ST.

W. WASHINGTON AVE.

Lake Monona

Henry Vilas Zoo

S. PARK ST.

BRITTINGHAM PARK

151

Henry Vilas Zoo

VILAS PARK DR.

Monona Bay

JOHN NOLEN DR.

Lake Wingra

151

MADISON
Downtown

The State Historical Museum presents Wisconsin's rich history, from the time of prehistoric Native Americans to the present. At the Wisconsin Veterans Museum you can learn about Wisconsin's military history. And the Madison Children's Museum has hands-on exhibits where you can see what it's like to go on an archaeological dig, plant and harvest crops, and even milk a cow.

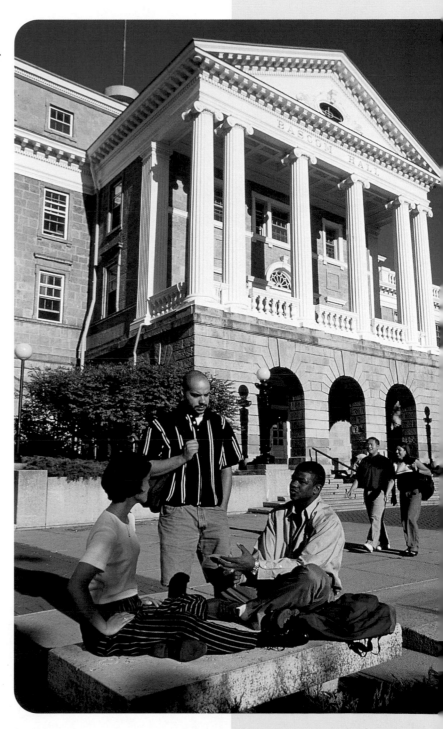

The University of Wisconsin was founded in 1848. Today, more than 40,000 students attend the university.

CHAPTER FIVE

THE PEOPLE AND PLACES OF WISCONSIN

The Milwaukee River Walk is a great place to walk, talk, eat, drink, boat, and play by the water.

Polish Americans in Milwaukee celebrate their culture at Polish Fest.

Wisconsin is the eighteenth largest state in population, with more than five million people. Nine out of every ten Wisconsinites are of European descent. Almost six of every hundred are African-American, and six of every hundred people are Asian, Native American, or Hispanic.

Many nationalities are represented throughout the state. Germans are the largest ethnic group, followed by Irish, Poles, Scandinavians, and British. Since 1990, Wisconsin's Hispanic population has doubled. The number of Asians has also increased by more than half during the 1990s. Large numbers of Hmong, Vietnamese, Laotians, and other Asians live in Wisconsin. As a matter of fact, Wisconsin has one of the largest groups of Hmong people in the United States. There are eleven American Indian nations in Wisconsin, with a total population of more than 40,000.

WORKING IN WISCONSIN

Wisconsin is one of the largest manufacturing states in the nation. More than 600,000 people in Wisconsin work in manufacturing. Milwaukee is the main manufacturing center. Manufacturing is also found in small and mid-sized cities throughout the state. In Milwaukee, a leading industry is the production of electronic equipment for health care. Several meat-packing industries are also in Milwaukee, as well as Miller brewing company. Madison's manufacturing businesses are food products, machinery, and medical equipment.

The Fox Valley in eastern Wisconsin is a major manufacturing center. Green Bay is a shipping port. There are also several meatpacking plants and large paper mills in the Green Bay area, which is how the city earned its nickname, "the toilet paper capital of the world." Racine and Kenosha are both ports and industrial cities on Lake Michigan, as well. Eau Claire is known for its paper factories as well as for its computer and technology industries.

People in the southern and eastern parts of the state work in agricultural industries, as well as manufacturing. Wisconsin's most famous exports are its dairy products. It ranks second among the states in the

The world's best dairy cattle compete in breeding shows at the World Dairy Expo in Madison.

number of dairy cows. It is also second, behind California, in the production of milk. Wisconsin leads the states in the production of cheese.

Of the 76,000 farms in Wisconsin, about 30,000 specialize in dairying. Other farms produce crops such as corn, hay, potatoes, and soybeans. Wisconsin is also one of the leading producers of canned vegetables. The Door County Peninsula is Wisconsin's leading fruit-growing area and is especially noted for its cherries. Sturgeon Bay is also a leading cherry-producing center. In the central regions of Wisconsin, cranberry growers harvest more than two million barrels of cranberries a year.

You can tour a cranberry marsh to see cranberries being harvested.

Lake Superior

50 mi.
0   25
0   25   50 km

Bayfield

MINNESOTA

MICHIGAN

Eau Claire

Wausau

Green
Bay

N

Lake
Michigan

Prairie du Chien

Madison ✪

Milwaukee

Racine

Kenosha

IOWA

ILLINOIS

Cattle
Corn
Cranberries
Dairy
Fish
Fruit
Hay
Hogs
Lead
Limestone

Manufacturing
Oats
Potatoes
Poultry
Sheep
Soybeans
Tobacco
Tourism
Vegetables

Tourism, the business of providing food, shelter, and entertainment for visitors, has become a major industry for the state. It brings in more than $12.8 billion a year and employs more than 177,000 people. The northern Wisconsin forest and lake country areas support a particularly large tourist and recreational industry.

The rest of the state's population works in service industries such as banks, retail stores, real estate, medicine, and schools. Recently, the most growth in state employment has been in the fields of nursing, computer programming, and recycling—the business of reusing material that has been discarded.

More than 10,000 people in Wisconsin work in the mining industry. Lead and zinc are still mined, but the main mining industry is in sandstone, limestone, quartzite, and silica sand. Wisconsin is the second-largest producer of rough stone used for buildings.

TAKE A TOUR OF WISCONSIN

Northeast Wisconsin

Let's start our tour in northeastern Wisconsin at Nicolet National Forest. Jean Nicolet explored this beautiful spot over 300 years ago, and today it is a huge forest that spreads out over 657,520 acres (266,089 hectares). You can enjoy a day of fishing or boating on one of the forest's 1,200 lakes, or go hiking on one of the many trails throughout the forest.

Marinette County in northern Wisconsin is known as Wisconsin's Waterfall Capital. It has more than a dozen waterfalls where you can go camping, hiking, and swimming. The upper part of the Peshtigo River is known as Roaring Rapids, and is famous for its white-water rafting and kayaking.

Also in northeastern Wisconsin is Eagle River, the Snowmobile Capital of the World. Every year the town hosts two of the most popular races in the sport. If you visit Eagle River during the winter, you'll see the famous Ice Palace made of 2,750 huge blocks of ice.

Southwest of Eagle River is Rhinelander, nicknamed the Hodag Town. In the 1800s, lumbermen told fantastic stories about a monster called the Hodag. The ferocious monster, said to be a hairy animal with horns and tusks, turned out to be a hoax. The Hodag had already become a popular local legend, however, and today Rhinelander holds a celebration called the Hodag Festival every year.

Wisconsin is home to the largest number of American Indian groups east of the Mississippi River. The northeast region includes the reservations and some trust-lands of the Forest County Potawatomis, the Mohican Nation (Stockbridge-Munsee Band), the Ho-Chunk Nation (Winnebago), the Menominees, the Oneidas, and the Sokaogon Ojibwe. Native American history can be explored in museums such as the Oneida Nation Museum in DePere. The Oneida museum has one of the largest exhibits of Oneida history and artifacts in the world.

Traditional Native American dance festivals are held every year in Wisconsin.

Devoted fans flock to Lambeau Field to watch the Green Bay Packers play football.

WHO'S WHO IN WISCONSIN?

Vince Lombardi (1913–1970) coached the Green Bay Packers from 1959 to 1968. He was one of the most famous professional football coaches in the country. He led the Packers to win three consecutive NFL titles in 1965, 1966, and 1967.

East Central Wisconsin

One of Wisconsin's oldest communities is Green Bay. It is located in the southern part of a bay with the same name. If you like football, visit the Green Bay Packer Hall of Fame, where you can find out all about the city's legendary Green Bay Packers football team.

The National Railroad Museum in Green Bay has seventy historical trains on display. Overlooking the Fox River is Heritage Hill State Park. At this living history museum you can experience life as it was in northeast Wisconsin more than a hundred years ago.

Jutting up from Green Bay is the Door Peninsula, home to five state parks. The best known is Peninsula State Park in Fish Creek. It is one of Wisconsin's oldest and largest state parks. The Cana Island Lighthouse is a popular attraction. The Door County Maritime Museum shows the shipbuilding history of the area and features exhibits on shipwrecks that have occurred in Lake Michigan and Lake Superior.

Discover the world of magic at the Houdini Historical Center in Appleton. Here you can find out about America's most famous magician, Harry Houdini. There's a great collection of the unusual things he used in his magic acts, including handcuffs, lock picks, and straitjackets.

Southeast Wisconsin

The southeastern section of Wisconsin has the largest city in the state, Milwaukee. Located on the shore of Lake Michigan, the city has many beaches and parks. It's also home to the Milwaukee Bucks basketball team and the Milwaukee Brewers baseball team. Baseball fans can watch Brewers games no matter what the weather—the motorized stadium roof at Miller Park opens and closes in a matter of minutes.

There's plenty to see and do in Milwaukee. The Milwaukee Public Museum is one of the nation's best natural-history and science museums. You can walk through a tropical rain forest, visit China or Africa (without getting on an airplane!), or get a close-up view of life beneath the ocean's surface. Also in Milwaukee is the Pettit National Ice Center, the largest ice arena in the nation. The Pettit serves as the official training facility for new members of the United States Olympic Speedskating Team.

If you love the circus, don't miss the Great Circus Parade. It is held once a year in downtown Milwaukee. This magnificent street parade features clowns, bands, historic circus wagons, and exotic animals. Another Milwaukee celebration is Summerfest, one of the world's

WHO'S WHO IN WISCONSIN?

Harry Houdini (1874–1926) was a famous magician who was well known for his escape tricks. His stunts included escaping from locked boxes while he was chained and handcuffed. He once escaped from a locked box that was dropped into a river. He lived in Appleton, Wisconsin.

Lake Superior

APOSTLE ISLANDS
NATIONAL
LAKESHORE

• Bayfield

MINNESOTA

MICHIGAN

ST. CROIX

NATIONAL

SCENIC

RIVERWAY

CHEQUAMEGON

NATIONAL

FOREST

8

NICOLET
NATIONAL
FOREST

51

8

141

• Wausau

• Eau Claire

94

NECEDAH NATIONAL
WILDLIFE REFUGE

39

51

Green Bay

TREMPEALEAU
NATIONAL
WILDLIFE REFUGE

90

90

94

43

HORICON
NATIONAL
WILDLIFE
REFUGE

Lake
Michigan

IOWA

Prairie du Chien

Madison ✪

94

Milwaukee

51

39

43

Lake
Geneva

94

• Racine

90

• Kenosha

ILLINOIS

National forest, lakeshore, wildlife
refuge, or scenic riverway

Highway

✪ Capital city

• City

■ Tourist site

0   25   50 mi.

0   25   50 km

N

largest music festivals. Every year nearly one million people come to enjoy live music and entertainment.

If you'd like to find out more about the ethnic history of Wisconsin, visit Old World Wisconsin in Eagle, a short drive from Milwaukee. This 1870s village tells the story of Wisconsin's history of immigration. Then make a stop in nearby Racine, which has a large Danish population. Racine is famous for its kringle, a delicious Danish pastry that is found in bakeries throughout the city.

As in other parts of the state, there are many nature areas. The largest freshwater cattail marsh in the country is Horicon Marsh. Each fall, more than 200,000 birds stop there on their way south for the winter.

Southwest Wisconsin

A large part of Wisconsin's history began in the southwestern corner of the state. During the mining days of the 1800s, Mineral Point was an important town in Wisconsin's mining district. Pendarvis, a state historic site in Mineral Point, still has log-and-limestone cottages where miners from Cornwall, England lived. Several of the area's mining museums also offer guided underground tours of old mines.

The cheesemaking industry also began in the southwest. The city of Monroe is the state's top cheese producer. Every summer, it hosts a big cheese festival called Cheese Days. Another big cheese city is New Glarus, where you can tour several large cheese factories. The Swiss Historical Village Museum offers a look at early Swiss pioneer life in Wisconsin.

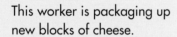

This worker is packaging up new blocks of cheese.

WHO'S WHO IN WISCONSIN?

John Muir (1838–1914) was a naturalist who campaigned for the conservation of land, water, and forests in the United States. He founded the Sierra Club, an important conservation organization, and helped to found Yosemite and Sequoia national parks in California. He grew up on a farm near Portage.

The southwest region of Wisconsin has some of the most beautiful nature areas in the state, and many state parks. The John Muir State Park near Madison is named for John Muir, one of the most famous naturalists in the world.

There are some large wildlife refuges in the area. The International Crane Foundation in Baraboo is home to fifteen species of crane, including the rare whooping crane and the six-foot-tall (2-m) sarus crane. The foundation is the world's center for the study and preservation of cranes.

The International Crane Foundation has helped save whooping cranes, which were once very close to extinction, through study and preservation.

A short drive from Madison is Little Norway, an outdoor museum that includes a collection of Norwegian antiques. You'll step back into the days of the settlers and discover some interesting things about the culture of the Norwegian people.

Nearby Wisconsin Dells is a scenic river gorge that has become one of the most popular tourist spots in the midwest. Rivers, wildlife areas, and hiking and biking trails provide all kinds of exciting outdoor entertainment. There are also indoor waterparks, antique shops, concerts, and museums, too. A fun place to visit in the Dells is Tommy Bartlett's Robot World & Exploratory, which has interactive exhibits, including an original Russian space station.

South of the Dells is Baraboo, where the famous Ringling Brothers Circus began in 1884. The Circus World Museum in Baraboo is the world's largest circus history museum, with more than fifty acres (20 hectares) of shows and exhibits.

Antique circus wagons like this one are on display at the Circus World Museum.

For a twist on ordinary pancakes try this Wisconsin recipe. It adds a Norwegian touch, making a tasty Wisconsin and Norwegian dish.

NORWEGIAN PANCAKES

(Makes about 30 five-inch-diameter pancakes)
6 large eggs
1 cup half-and-half
3 cups milk
2 cups flour
2 tbsp. sugar
1/2 tsp. salt
1/8 tsp. grated nutmeg
1 cup (2 sticks) butter, melted
cranberries or strawberries
sweetened whipped cream

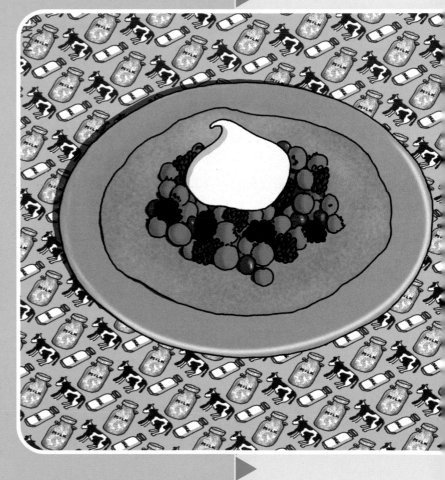

1. Beat the eggs in a large mixing bowl for about a minute. Add the half-and-half and milk. Beat them together.
2. Mix the flour, sugar, salt and nutmeg together. Add the mixture to the liquid ingredients and beat for 30 seconds.
3. Gradually stir in the melted butter.
4. Using about 1/3 cup of batter for each pancake, pour the batter onto an ungreased hot griddle or nonstick frying pan. Fry pancakes until the edges look dry and cooked, about 1 minute. Flip the pancake and fry for about 30 seconds, until edges are lightly browned.
5. Serve each pancake topped with berries and a spoonful of whipped cream.

Northwest Wisconsin

Northwest Wisconsin has dramatic landscapes that were created by glaciers. The Ice Age National Scenic Trail is a 1,200-mile (1,931-km) walking/hiking trail that stretches across Wisconsin, with a 40-mile (64-km) stretch passing through this part of the state. Many land features along the trail were formed as a result of the Ice Age.

The Great Divide Scenic Byway winds its way through the Chequamegon-Nicolet National Forest and offers some of the best views anywhere. The Chequamegon side is more than 857,000 acres (346,816 hectares), with many spectacular waterfalls and canyons.

The Apostle Islands National Lakeshore on Lake Superior features long stretches of sandy beaches, cool sea caves, and ancient forests. It also has the largest collection of lighthouses anywhere in the National Park System.

Near the Mississippi River is Pepin, the birthplace of Laura Ingalls Wilder. The Laura Ingalls Wilder Wayside & Cabin is a replica of her childhood home, and the Pepin Historical Museum has local history and information about this famous writer.

WHO'S WHO IN WISCONSIN?

Laura Ingalls Wilder (1867–1957) was a children's book author. She wrote the *Little House* series about Wisconsin and Midwest frontier life. Wilder based her stories on her own life in Wisconsin and other parts of the Midwest.

(opposite)
The Ice Age National Scenic Trail follows the hills that were left behind by the glaciers over 10,000 years ago.

WISCONSIN ALMANAC

Statehood date and number: May 29, 1848/30th

State seal: Created in 1881; includes the state coat of arms, which also appears on the state flag

State flag: Approved by the legislature on April 26, 1913

Geographic center: Wood County, 9 miles (14 km) southeast of Marshfield

Total area/rank: 65,498 square miles (169,639 sq km)/22nd

Coastline: About 800 miles (1,287 km)

Borders: Lake Superior, Michigan, Illinois, Lake Michigan, Iowa, Minnesota

Latitude and longitude: Wisconsin is located approximately between 42° 30' and 47° 3' N and 86° 49' and 92° 54' W

Highest/lowest elevation: Timms Hill, 1,952 feet (595 m)/shore of Lake Michigan, 581 feet (177 m)

Hottest/coldest temperature: 114°F (45.6°C) at Wisconsin Dells on July 14, 1936/-54°F (-47.8°C) at Danbury on January 24, 1922

Land area/rank: 54,310 square miles (140, 663 sq km)/25th

Inland water area: 1,830 square miles (4,740 sq km)

Population/rank: (2000 census) 5,363,675/18th

Population of major cities:
   Milwaukee: 596,974
   Madison: 208,054
   Green Bay: 102,313
   Kenosha: 90,352
   Racine: 81,855

Greatest distance north to south: 320 miles (512 km)

Greatest distance east to west: 295 miles (472 km)

Origin of state name: Based on the Algonquian language word *Ouisconsin*, believed to mean "grassy place," "gathering of the waters," or "place of the beaver"

State capital: Madison

Previous capitals: Belmont (Territory of Wisconsin) until 1838

Counties: 72

State government: 33 senators, 99 assembly members

Major rivers and lakes: Mississippi River, Wisconsin River, Fox River, Rock River, Lake Michigan, Lake Superior, Lake Winnebago, Lake Pepin, Lake Geneva

Farm products: Milk, cheese, corn, snap beans, peas, beets, potatoes, oats, hay, cherries, and cranberries

Livestock: Cattle/calves, sheep/lambs, hogs/pigs, chickens

Manufactured products: Automobiles, machinery, furniture, medical equipment, paper, beer, and processed foods

Mining products: Granite, sandstone, limestone, copper, iron ore, and lead

Fishing products: Walleye pike, trout, muskellunge, perch, crappie, and bass

Animal: Badger

Beverage: Milk

Bird: Robin

Dance: Polka

Dog: American water spaniel

Domestic animal: Dairy cow

Fish: Muskie (muskellunge)

Flower: Wood violet

Fossil: Trilobite

Grain: Corn

Insect: Honey bee

Mineral: Galena (lead)

Motto: Forward

Nickname: Badger State

Rock: Red granite

Soil: Antigo silt loam

Song: "On Wisconsin," music composed by William T. Purdy; written by J. S. Hubbard and Charles D. Rosa

State fairs: State Fair Park, West Allis

Tree: Sugar maple

Wild animal: White-tailed deer

Wildlife: White-tailed deer, elk, muskrat, woodchuck, wolves, red fox, coyote, skunk, raccoon, mink, otter, beaver, badger, cottontail rabbit, black bear, and squirrel

TIMELINE

WISCONSIN STATE HISTORY

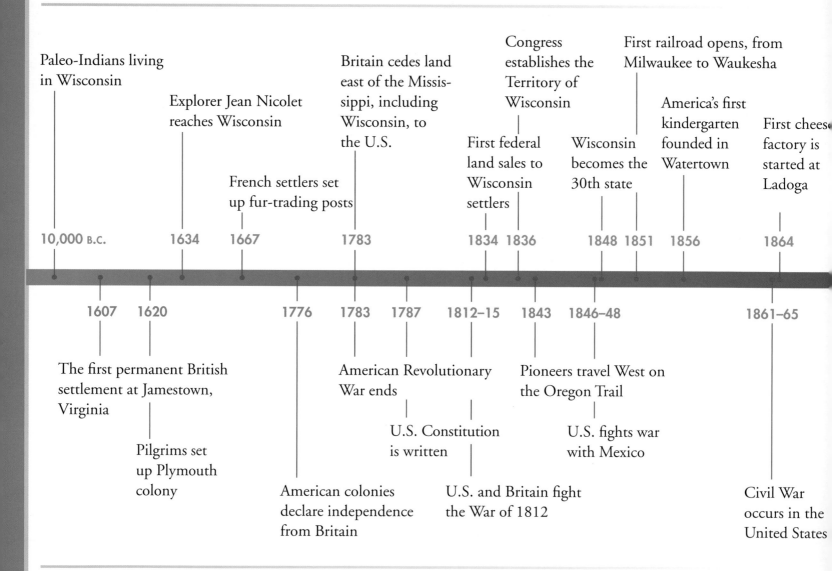

Paleo-Indians living
in Wisconsin

Explorer Jean Nicolet
reaches Wisconsin

Britain cedes land
east of the Missis-
sippi, including
Wisconsin, to
the U.S.

Congress
establishes the
Territory of
Wisconsin

First railroad opens, from
Milwaukee to Waukesha

First federal
land sales to
Wisconsin
settlers

Wisconsin
becomes the
30th state

America's first
kindergarten
founded in
Watertown

First chees-
factory is
started at
Ladoga

French settlers set
up fur-trading posts

| 10,000 B.C. | 1634 | 1667 | 1783 | 1834 | 1836 | 1848 | 1851 | 1856 | 1864 |

| 1607 | 1620 | 1776 | 1783 | 1787 | 1812–15 | 1843 | 1846–48 | 1861–65 |

The first permanent British
settlement at Jamestown,
Virginia

American Revolutionary
War ends

Pioneers travel West on
the Oregon Trail

Pilgrims set
up Plymouth
colony

U.S. Constitution
is written

U.S. fights war
with Mexico

American colonies
declare independence
from Britain

U.S. and Britain fight
the War of 1812

Civil War
occurs in the
United States

UNITED STATES HISTORY

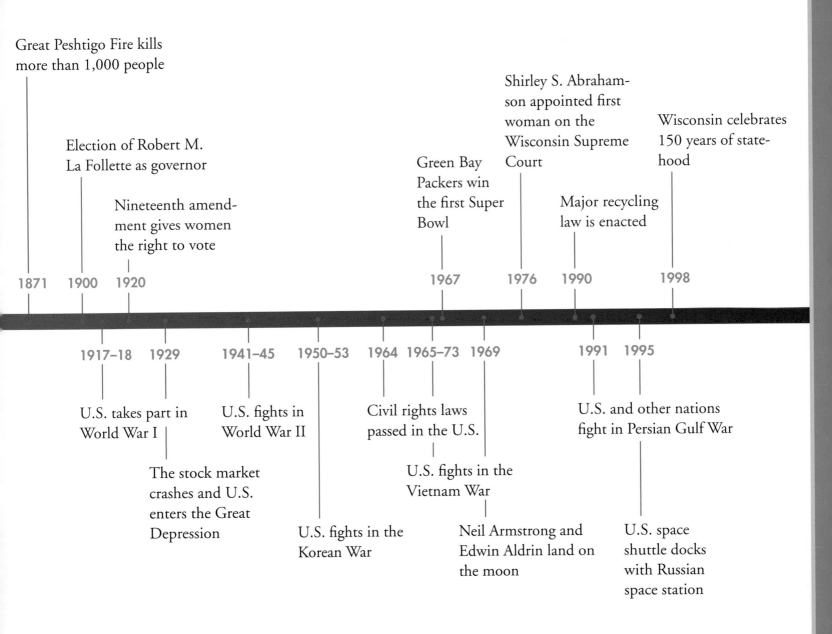

Great Peshtigo Fire kills more than 1,000 people

Election of Robert M. La Follette as governor

Nineteenth amendment gives women the right to vote

Green Bay Packers win the first Super Bowl

Shirley S. Abrahamson appointed first woman on the Wisconsin Supreme Court

Major recycling law is enacted

Wisconsin celebrates 150 years of statehood

1871 1900 1920   1967   1976 1990   1998

1917–18 1929   1941–45 1950–53 1964 1965–73 1969   1991 1995

U.S. takes part in World War I

U.S. fights in World War II

Civil rights laws passed in the U.S.

U.S. and other nations fight in Persian Gulf War

The stock market crashes and U.S. enters the Great Depression

U.S. fights in the Vietnam War

U.S. fights in the Korean War

Neil Armstrong and Edwin Aldrin land on the moon

U.S. space shuttle docks with Russian space station

GALLERY OF FAMOUS WISCONSINITES

Shirley S. Abrahamson
(1933–)
Chief Justice of the Wisconsin Supreme Court. She was appointed in 1976, becoming the first and only woman to serve on the court until 1993.

Eric Heiden
(1958–)
Olympic gold medalist in speedskating. Won a record five gold medals in the 1980 Winter Olympics. His record still holds today as the most gold medals won at any sport in the Winter Olympics. Born in Madison.

Elroy "Crazy Legs" Hirsch
(1923–2004)
Football star who played for the University of Wisconsin-Madison and the Los Angeles Rams. Admitted to the Football Hall of Fame.

Aldo Leopold
(1887–1948)
One of the founders of the environmental movement in the United States. He taught wildlife management at the University of Wisconsin.

Georgia O'Keeffe
(1887–1986)
Artist famous for her imaginative paintings of flowers and landscapes. Awarded the Presidential Medal of Freedom in 1977. Born in Sun Prairie.

Vel Phillips
(1924–)
The first African-American and the first woman to be elected to the Milwaukee Common Council. Born in Milwaukee.

George C. Poage
(1880–1962)
The first African-American athlete to compete in the modern Olympics. Poage won two bronze medals in the 1904 Olympics at St. Louis. He was born in Wisconsin.

Mitchell Red Cloud, Jr.
(1924–1950)
A Ho-Chunk who was awarded the Congressional Medal of Honor for his service in the Korean War, becoming the first Ho-Chunk to be so honored. Born in Hatfield.

Thornton N. Wilder
(1897–1975)
Playwright and novelist who received the Pulitzer Prize for three works: the novel *The Bridge of San Luis Rey,* and the plays *Our Town* and *The Skin of Our Teeth.* Born in Madison.

GLOSSARY

abolish: to put an end to, or do away with

artifact: object from the past that was made or changed by human beings, such as a tool

constitution: document that outlines the laws or principles by which a nation, government, or group is organized

controversy: public dispute between two sides holding opposite views

demonstration: rally or march held to express a public opinion

discriminate: to show preference to a certain people based on their belonging to a class or category

economy: use or management of resources, such as money, materials, or labor

emigrant: person who leaves one country or region to settle in another

ethnic: group of people sharing a common racial, national, religious, or cultural heritage

extinct: no longer in existence

gorge: deep narrow passage with steep rocky sides, often with a stream flowing through it

immigrant: person who enters a country of which they are not native to live in it permanently

kettles: water-filled pits formed by blocks of glacial ice that were left behind

limestone: hard rock, formed from the remains of shells or coral, that is used in building

moraine: soil, rocks, and debris that collect at the edges of and underneath a glacier

mural: a large picture applied directly to a wall or ceiling

peninsula: piece of land that sticks out into a body of water and is surrounded by water on three sides

revolution: rebellion by the people of a country against their government to change the system under which they have been ruled

sandstone: sedimentary rock made up usually of quartz sand mixed with some kind of cement

sedimentation: soil, sand, and stones left by water runoff in rivers, harbors, and lakes

segregation: act of separating people from society based on race or class

treaty: formal agreement outlining terms of peace or trade

FOR MORE INFORMATION

Web sites

The State Historical Society of Wisconsin
http://www.shsw.wisc.edu/
History of Wisconsin; links to other Wisconsin history sites

Wisconsin: Celebrating People, Place, and Past
http://www.ecb.org/wisconsin/
Historical information on Wisconsin

State of Wisconsin Information Server
http://www.wisconsin.gov/state/home
General Wisconsin information; links to Wisconsin Web sites

Wisconsin Department of Tourism
http://www.travelwisconsin.com
Information on historical sites, parks, nature areas, and unusual places to visit

Wisconsin Maps
http://www.wisconline.com/maps/
Current and historical maps of Wisconsin

Books

Bial, Raymond. *Portrait of a Farm Family.* New York, NY: Houghton Mifflin, 1995.

Cha, Dia. *Dia's Story Cloth: The Hmong People's Journey of Freedom.* New York, NY: Lee and Low Bks., 1998.

Thorne-Thomsen, Kathleen. *Frank Lloyd Wright for Kids: His Life and Ideas.* Chicago, IL: Chicago Review Press, 1994.

Walker, Barbara M. *The Little House Cookbook: Frontier Foods from Laura Ingalls Wilder's Classic Stories.* New York, NY: HarperCollins, 1995.

Addresses

State Historical Society of Wisconsin
816 State St.
Madison, WI 53706

Office of the Governor
115 East State Capitol
Madison, WI 53702

INDEX

ABOUT THE AUTHOR

Bettina Ling has been a children's book writer, editor, and author of educational materials for more than fifteen years. She is the author of thirteen books for children and young adults. Writing this book has been especially meaningful for Bettina, since she lived for five years in Milwaukee and spent every summer of her childhood swimming, waterskiing, and fishing in Eagle River, Wisconsin. She received much support from her favorite Wisconsinite, her brother John, in the writing of this book.